Instant New York City

GW00492606

APA PUBLICATIONS

Part of the Langenscheidt Publishing Group

CONTENTS

Compiled by Martha Ellen Zenfell
Photography by Tony Perrottet
Cover photograph: Image Bank

All Rights Reserved
First Edition 2001

As every effort is made to provide accu-
rate information in this publication, we
would appreciate it if readers would call
our attention to any errors that may occur
by communicating with Apa Publications,
PO Box 7910, London SE1 1WE,
England. Fax: (44) 20 7403 0290;
e-mail: insight@apaguide.demon.co.uk

Distributed in the UK & Ireland by
GeoCenter International Ltd
The Viables Centre, Harrow Way
Basingstoke, Hampshire RG22 4BJ
Fax: (44 1256) 817-988

Distributed in the United States by
Langenscheidt Publishers, Inc.
46–35 54th Road, Maspeth, NY 11378
Tel: (718) 784-0055. Fax: (718) 784-0640

Worldwide distribution enquiries:
APA Publications GmbH & Co. Verlag KG
Singapore Branch, Singapore
38 Joo Koon Road, Singapore 628990
Tel: (65) 865-1600. Fax: (65) 861-6438

Printed in Singapore by
Insight Print Services (Pte) Ltd
38 Joo Koon Road, Singapore 628990
Tel: (65) 865-1600. Fax: (65) 861-6438

www.insightguides.com

THE BIG APPLE

Born from a steal of a real estate deal – for a box of trinkets worth $24 – between the Dutch and the local Algonquin Indians, New York now has some of the most expensive real estate in the world. Today, in the frantic world of downtown Manhattan, $24 buys about half a square inch of office space – maybe even less. The entire city covers a surface area of 301 sq. miles (780 sq. km). Of its five boroughs, only the Bronx lies on the mainland; Manhattan and Staten Island are islands, while Brooklyn and Queens form the westernmost point of Long Island. Manhattan, the smallest borough, has a surface area of just over 22 sq. miles (57 sq. km), but is the most densely populated part of the city, with about 1.5 million of the city's total 7.4 million inhabitants.

In addition, almost 40 million people travel to New York every year; it's the most visited city in the world. Visitors will be soothed to know that, despite its history as a hotbed of crime (organized, petty and otherwise), a recent FBI report says that New York has the lowest crime rate in the US's top 25 cities.

There are a few things you can always count on: world-class museums, a wild array of shops, stunning architecture, great entertainment, earth-shattering business deals, outrageous street life and a frenzied non-stop personal rhythm. This is a city about living and change, excitement and struggle.

Left: the Statue of Liberty

"What is barely hinted at in other American cities is condensed and enlarged in New York," said the writer Saul Bellow. True enough. Culturally, New York has more than 150 museums, including some of the largest in the world (the Metropolitan Museum of Art), around 400 art galleries and more than 240 theaters. Broadway and the Metropolitan Opera are famous the world over.

The entertainment possibilities in "the city that never sleeps" are immense: there's a choice of over 60 clubs, offering everything from jazz to blues to salsa, and hundreds of places to dance every night of the week. Hungry? Select from more than 17,000 different places to eat, from kosher to kitsch to haute cuisine. Amid all the bustle, there are quiet places too: the city has over 26,000 acres (10,500 hectares) of parks, the most notable of which is Central Park.

Above: *Orchard Street market on the Lower East Side*

But it's the New Yorkers themselves who make this city so exciting. There is a good reason why such well-known publicity-shy figures as Greta Garbo and Jacqueline Onassis called New York "home". It's the same reason that might inspire any number of people to pack their bags and head here some day; some of them for good. New York is the place where ordinary people can, if they are willing to be lucky, become stars, by performing in Washington Square Park, or by making it big in business, on Wall Street or in the media; it's also the place where real stars can walk down the street unnoticed. Or so we are led to believe: New York is the city of myths, and making them, telling them, or repeating them is a part of it.

Fast-paced Town

Despite the recent "let's be polite" campaign that came into effect near the turn of the millennium, New York is a fast-paced town whose residents are possessed of a restless energy. Few people seem to have time for anything not on their mental sched-ule; even asking for directions in the street is best done with an awareness of this – ideally, while moving at the same pace and in the same direc-tion as the informant.

New Yorkers have persuaded themselves that liv-ing at breakneck speed, under constant and intense pressure, is stimulating. This is what gives them the edge and makes Manhattan the center of the uni-verse. Which – as we know – all New Yorkers believe implicitly.

Right: *rollerblading in Central Park*

HISTORICAL HIGHLIGHTS

1000–1500 Algonquin tribes hunt for animals on the island later known as Manhattan.

1609 Englishman Henry Hudson weighs anchor on the island, then sails the *Half Moon* up the river that now bears his name.

1624 The Dutch West India Company establishes a trading post at the south tip of the island, the current site of Battery Park.

1626 The provincial director general of the New Amsterdam settlement, Peter Minuit, purchases Manhattan from the local Indians for 60 guilders' worth of trinkets – the equivalent of $24.

1630s Dutch farmers settle in what is now Brooklyn and the Bronx.

1664 In the first year of the sea war between Britain and Holland, director general Peter Stuyvesant is forced to surrender the town to the British without a fight. New Amsterdam is renamed New York, after King Charles II's brother, James, Duke of York.

1690 With a population of 3,900, New York is the third-largest town in North America.

1765 In accordance with the Stamp Act, unfair taxes are levied against the colonists.

1770 A series of skirmishes between the Sons of Liberty and British soldiers culminate in the Battle of Golden Hill.

1776 The Revolutionary War begins and the colonies declare their independence from Great

Left: George Washington

Britain. George Washington, in command of the colonial troops, loses the Battle of Long Island. British troops occupy New York until 1783.

1789 New York becomes capital of the newly founded United States of America, but only retains this status briefly.

1789 George Washington is inaugurated at the site of the Federal Hall, Wall Street.

1811 An important decision is made affecting the city's future appearance: all streets are to be laid out in the form of a grid.

1820 An official Stock Exchange replaces an outdoor money market on Wall Street.

1825 The Erie Canal, linking the Hudson River with the Great Lakes, boosts the economy.

1830 Irish and German immigrants begin arriving in great numbers. The city's population soon tops 200,000.

1835 Manhattan between South Broad and Wall Street is ravaged by the "Great Fire".

1857 William Marcy, also known as "Boss" Tweed, is elected to the County Board of Supervisors and launches a career of notorious corruption.

Above: *Lower Manhattan in the 1730s*

1858 Calvert Vaux and Frederick Law Olmsted submit plans for the city's Central Park.

1860 New York becomes the largest city in the US. Brooklyn's population increased 10 times in the past 30 years.

1861 The Civil War begins.

1877 The Museum of Natural History opens.

1880 The Metropolitan Museum of Art opens.

1883 Brooklyn Bridge officially opens. First performance is held at the Metropolitan Opera.

1886 The Statue of Liberty is unveiled on Liberty Island.

1892 Ellis Island in New York Harbor becomes the point of entry for immigrants to the US.

1898 New York's five boroughs are united under one municipal government.

1904 A subway system is begun.

1913 Construction of the tallest skyscraper in the world, the Woolworth Buildings, begins.

1929 Wall Street crashes, and with it comes the start of the Great Depression.

1930 The Chrysler Building becomes the world's tallest skyscraper.

1931 The Empire State Building, the new "tallest", opens.

1933 Fiorello LaGuardia is elected mayor and uses federal money to fight the devastating effects of the Depression.

1939 Ten years after its foundation by Abby Aldrich Rockefeller, the Museum of Modern Art moves into its new home on 53rd Street.

1946 The United Nations begins meeting in New York. The permanent buildings on East 42nd–48th streets are opened in 1952.

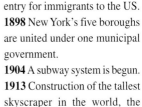

Left: Mayor Fiorello LaGuardia

1959 The Guggenheim Museum opens its doors for the first time. Work begins on Lincoln Center.
1965 A 16-hour-long power cut brings the city to a standstill.
1973 World Trade Center opens.
1975 As the city financial crisis deepens, the US government bails New York out with a loan.
1983 Trump Tower is completed on Fifth Avenue.
1993 A bomb explodes below the World Trade Center. Many are injured.
1993 Rudolph Giuliani, a former prosecutor, is elected mayor.
1997 Giuliani is re-elected. His "get tough on crime" campaign is proven highly effective, and the Big Apple becomes one of the safer large cities in the US.
1998 Citywide celebrations of the Centennial of Greater New York, marking the amalgamation of the five boroughs.
2000 Giuliani runs against US First Lady Hillary Rodham Clinton in a bid to become Senator for New York state, only to pull out due to ill health.
2001 The high-profile Clinton takes up office as Senator, after defeating new Republican candidate Rick Lazio.

Above: Brooklyn Bridge footpath in 1923

PEOPLE AND CULTURE

In Spanish they call it *corazon*. In Yiddish, it's *chutzpah*. Guts, spirit, heart, call it what you want, New Yorkers have got it. Just watch the parade of humanity that animates every street of New York City. Hip teen gangs and chic male models, aging eccentrics and world-weary young beauties, macho Puerto Rican studs in muscle shirts and sourfaced society matrons in furs, sassy loudmouthed schoolgirls, dignified Chinese grandmothers, elegant black women with attaché cases – every face is charged with personality and a daring that comes from a strong sense of self.

So, which face in this crowd is the quintessential New Yorker – that charismatic individual who so deserves our time and respect? That's a trick question – the answer is: all of the above.

The New York Spirit

The New Yorker comes from every corner of the world, from every type of ethnic and economic background, from Sudanese poverty to Parisian glamor. But despite this diversity, there is a trait that all New Yorkers, natives and newcomers alike, share – the New York spirit – a certain scrappiness, a grim humor, a zest for life even in the face of adversity.

The crowd reveals the New York spirit by a flash of style, a brassy wit, a streetwise cosmopolitanism. New Yorkers breathe worldliness, toughness, tolerance and skepticism along with the smog: these traits are part of the city's vital culture. Through a brief and by no means complete survey of the literature of New York City through the centuries – from Henry James' *Washington Square* to Tom Wolfe's *Bonfire of the Vanities*, some of the

Left: *people and places in the Big Apple*

ethnicities and distinctive personalities behind the faces in the crowd emerge, as does, perhaps, the New York spirit.

It might sound trite, but New York City is a place where anything can happen, very good or very bad. And it usually does. It's a city dangerous with possibilities, a rollicking testimony to the creative powers of disorder and chaos.

Influence and Interest

It's not difficult to see why. Put 1½ million people on a tiny island and they're bound to kick up sparks. Add into the mix some of the world's most influential institutions, corporations, artists and thinkers – not to mention an immigrant population from every corner of the world – and the sparks ignite a bonfire. That's what makes it such an interesting place.

There are people who say that the glory days of New York are over, that it's all downhill from here. What they don't understand is that New York was born in the fire, the fire of ambition: if it happens anywhere, it will happen here. And yet the city

remains intangible, just out of grasp. Then the fact becomes apparent: as soon as you feel you understand New York, your understanding is obsolete.

The Melting Pot's Ingredients

"A map of the city colored to designate nationalities would show more stripes than on the skin of a zebra and more colors than any rainbow," wrote Jacob Riis in the early 1900s at the peak of the great tide of immigration that swept into the US – and the city – between 1840 and 1925.

And even though the descendants of those very immigrants might be fashion designers or CEOs of multi-national corporations, this factor is still very much a part of the fabric of the city.

The museum at Ellis Island in Lower Manhattan has ignited a resurgence of interest in preserving New York's pluralistic heritage. There, anyone can research an individual immigrant's journey from their homeland to the new world. People come from all over the globe to the Wall of Honor, inscribed with the names of thousands of immigrants.

Between 1830 and 1840, about 600,000 immigrants, largely from the British Isles (including Ireland), Germany and Scandinavia, landed in America. About 150,000 of these stayed in

*Left: New Year's Eve, Times Square **Above:** Ellis Island Museum*

New York City, while the rest fanned out to upstate New York, or to other parts of the country.

From 1840 to 1850, over 1,700,000 further foreigners arrived in New York. By 1849, the Irish made up nearly 50 percent of total immigration numbers. Scandinavians for the most part headed up the Hudson bound for the Midwest, but some found jobs in New York's shipping industry. German Jews came from 1820 to 1880, many becoming highly successful.

The next Jewish wave, some 2 million impoverished Europeans fleeing Russia, arrived between 1870 and 1914. In 1880 came millions of Slavs and Italians. The floodgates were open and in they flowed. Exclusion policies restricted Asians for a time but eventually their numbers also swelled New York's ranks, so much so in recent years that now Asian shopkeepers, florists and, especially, taxi drivers are among the most visible of all the immigrant groups.

Above: the story of New York's immigration is told here

The Birth of Harlem

Many immigrants of West Indian origin entered New York as "involuntary immigrants" – that is, brought in by the Dutch as slave labor. Their labor built much of early New Amsterdam, as New York was called. Much later, in the 1910 migration, blacks from the Southern states traveled north in search of work. Harlem, once exclusively white, became an African-American community and soon "the Negro capital of the world."

Mass immigration to the city itself, particularly during the late 19th and early 20th centuries, crammed tenements and sweat shops with more people than they could handle.

Caribbean Islanders began to join the state population in the 1940s, drawn by wartime jobs; the area known as Spanish Harlem on New York's Upper East Side became their community.

After World War II, with public services at an all-time high and its tax base weakened, the city was in a financial stranglehold. The situation was exacerbated by high-level corruption, with organized crime infiltrating government.

During the early 1950s, more than 1,000 Puerto Ricans a week arrived in New York City. Immigrants and refugees continued to arrive from around the globe, subtly changing the city: around 35 percent of today's population were born overseas. But the old image of impoverished immigrants is now largely out of date.

Above: bargains in Harlem

Many nationalities that have come to New York have made the fortunes that they initially dreamed of. Some Koreans and Pakistanis running stores or driving yellow cabs are saving so that they can leave the city to settle in a quieter community upstate. At the other end of the spectrum are the fourth generations descended from immigrants, thriving in pleasant communities on Long Island, or making their own mark in the great metropolis, where the immigrant experience began.

Culture and the City

The intellectual and artistic life of the city has its rituals, like museum openings, and its own venues. There are professional philosophers and critics who by their presence give definition to the proper noun New York Intellectual. But those people and places represent only the surface stratum of something deeper.

It represents a range of mental endeavor – Sinology and sculpture, poetry and particle physics – and it is a rich and polyglot marketplace of lectures, galleries, museums, plays, concerts,

libraries, films and, of course, dinner parties. It is the casual way great minds have always moved through the landscape: Thomas Wolfe stalking the streets of Brooklyn, Sonny Rollins practicing his saxophone on the Williamsburg Bridge. It is a painter named Mizue Sawano who used to go to the Brooklyn Botanic Garden once a week to sit with her easel beside the Lily Pools. The lily pads there reminded her of Monet's lily pads, she said, and they inspired her own art.

At the top of the New York economic scale, the captains of commerce and industry began to endow museums and to support individual artists; at the bottom, each wave of immigrants enriched and diversified the intellectual community.

Size and Sustenance

With size comes sustenance for all sorts of specialized intellectual communities. Greenwich Village became an urban version of the artists' colony, a home to creators of all stripes, the neighborhood that gave Eugene O'Neill a stage in the 1920s and Bob Dylan a bandstand in the 1960s. Miles uptown from the Village, Harlem has been home to a black intelligentsia that included writers Langston Hughes, James Weldon Johnson, James Baldwin and Ralph Ellison.

The notion of pop culture versus high culture is rendered almost meaningless, because the esoteric can enjoy a mass audience: such demanding playwrights and composers as Tom Stoppard and Stephen Sondheim can have hits on Broadway,

Left: half-price tickets from Times Square **Above:** street music

while a gospel-music version of Oedipus at Colonus – could anything seem more unlikely? – can be a sell-out at the Brooklyn Academy of Music.

This intellectual sweep allows almost unparalleled opportunities for eclecticism, for search and discovery. As buildings are torn down and replaced, or gutted and remodeled, artists are lured to New York by the change and variety, making it the major international center for the visual arts.

The City That Never Sleeps

New York is where you'll find Broadway, Radio City, Lincoln Center, Carnegie Hall and other major venues that have launched big names in theater, dance and music. Here also, on every street corner, are dreamers – talented students performing chamber music, an Ecuadorean folk band or a Caribbean musician play-

ing Bach on steel drums – all of them hoping for the big-time.

Some New Yorkers stick to mainstream theater for their culture, never going below 42nd Street. Others shun Broadway's extravagance or just can't afford it. But not all New York's culture has a hefty price tag. Outdoor performances of the New York Philharmonic, the Metropolitan Opera or the New York Shakespeare Festival are popular forms of fresh-air culture; not only that but they're also free of charge.

Left: *jazz in a Greenwich Village club*

New York's dance boom began in the 1960s, with an infusion of funding and the defection of Russian superstars Rudolf Nureyev, Mikhail Baryshnikov and Natalia Makarova. The legendary George Balanchine, one of the artistic giants of the 1900s, designed much of the performance space at Lincoln Center's New York State Theater, including a basket-weave dance floor to provide elasticity and minimize injury. The American Ballet Theater (ABT), which performs at Lincoln Center's Metropolitan Opera House, originally had a classical repertory, but under the direction of artistic director Mikhail Baryshnikov, began to offer works by contemporary choreographers.

Chilling Out

Not all culture is serious. Comedy clubs thrive all around town and, if you're lucky, you may catch Robin Williams or Rita Rudner working out new material. And for chilling out, where do New Yorkers go? To serious, smoky jazz clubs. To teenage discos. To rowdy Country & Western bars where Wall Street traders buy drinks for women who wistfully claim they once worked the Texas rodeos. To gay clubs. To places in Harlem, where whites go only when invited. To the Roxy, where rollerskating first found an indoor home. Or elegant hotel piano bars where couples with discretion can get romantic, or drunk, or both. Everybody in this town has his own parade.

Above: *Lincoln Center is the place for classical arts*

Media in Manhattan

Media in New York is a physical force, not a concept. If a savvy Manhattanite wants to get ahead, knowledge is power. For today's New Yorker, that translates into a willingness to be bombarded by information from around 50 radio stations, more than 100 television channels,and, of course, the Internet.

New York has the oldest continuously published daily newspaper in the country, *The New York Post*, as well as the highly regarded *New York Times* (of Times Square fame). There are over a dozen daily and weekly newspapers, plus hundreds of magazines and periodicals the voracious reader can buy at the Eastern Newstand in the MetLife Building above Grand Central Station. The best all-purpose local magazines are *New York*, the *New Yorker*, *Time Out New York* and others that demonstrate a commitment to "being on top of things," as do free weekly newspapers like the *Village Voice* and the *New York Press*.

Above: savvy New Yorkers have their pick of media information

Radio and Television

Radio especially lends itself to busy city life because listeners can do more than one thing at a time, important for multi-tasking New Yorkers. At any time of the day or night, radios are tuned to one of the city's commercial or non-commercial stations. It was radio that first introduced single-theme programming, a concept that now extends to cable TV and beyond. When a show like *Late Show with David Letterman* (taped on Broadway) goes to commercials, alternative viewing options range from NY-1, a station devoted to nonstop news *only* about New York, to national shows including *Today* (beamed from Rockefeller Center), *Good Morning America* and the local *Good Day New York*.

Hollywood on the Hudson

Ever since *The Lights of New York* was released in 1927, the city has been indelibly printed on the world's celluloid consciousness.

The most famous image is probably black-and-white King Kong atop the Empire State Building, filmed again (badly) in 1976.

The Empire struck back when New York writer-turned-director Nora Ephron made *Sleepless in Seattle*, itself a pastiche of the 1957 three-hankie weepie *An Affair to Remember*. Director Spike Lee vividly conveyed contemporary life Uptown in *Mo Better Blues*, while Greenwich Village has featured in everything from Fonda and Redford going *Barefoot in the Park* to Scorsese's

Right: *Marilyn gets the streetwise treatment*

Raging Bull (the swimming pool by St Luke's Place). *How to Marry a Millionaire* was set in between the two areas; the classy apartment rented by those sassy dames Monroe, Grable and Bacall is 36 Sutton Place South in Midtown. More than 200 films are made each year, many at the Kaufman Astoria Studios in Queens. The Astoria's most famous component is the American Museum of the Moving Image, the first institute in the US devoted to exploring the art, history, technique and technology of motion pictures, television and video.

American Museum of the Moving Image

Although not particularly glitzy or glam, AMOMI does have a pleasing archival feel about it, which befits a studio where both the Marx Brothers and Gloria Swanson worked. Film retrospectives are held here, in a variety of theaters. One is a 1960s-style living room with shag rug; another is an amusing homage to the lavish neo-Egyptian-style picture palaces of the 1920s.

Internationally, the filmmaker most indelibly associated with the city is Woody Allen. From *Annie Hall* and *Manhattan* to *Hannah and Her Sisters* and *Bullets Over Broadway*, nobody has portrayed modern New York (and his own personal neuroses) with more acuity and affection than Allen.

*Above: Woody Allen movie poster **Right:** food for thought*

Food

Fattening and fancy, or dished up fast to fuel the system, New York's food reads like a litany of all the immigrant groups who have arrived at the city's shores. Discerning diners can choose from Korean, Indian and Italian to French, Russian or Hungarian in their quest for treats to tickle the palate. Even the street food is good – those ubiquitous giant pretzels smothered in salt; the chestnuts roasting on a cold winter's day, or Nathans Famous Hot Dogs, which are worth traveling to Coney Island just to sample.

Restaurants appear and disappear with startling abruptness, victims of the city tendency to view "food as a fashion statement." But a few remain year in and year out, varying in quality but with enough pulling power to qualify as the *grande dames* of the dining table: if you can swing a reservation, you'll be able to tell your kids about it for decades. These include the Four Seasons with its famous Grill Room; Le Cirque, where the socialites go; Lutece, famed for its French food; and The River Café in Brooklyn, located on a barge with drop-dead gorgeous views of the Manhattan skyline.

New York's Green Spaces

In 1609, when Henry Hudson sailed the *Half Moon* up the river that was later named for him, Hudson's first mate wrote: "We found a land full of great tall oaks, with grass and flowers, as pleasant as ever has been seen." His words seem to echo when

taking a stroll through Central Park today. To landscape architect Frederick Law Olmsted, who designed it in the 1850s with Calvert Vaux, the purpose was to "supply hundreds of thousands of tired workers, who have no opportunity to spend summers in the country, a specimen of God's handiwork."

Springtime in New York

Central Park includes the largest stand of American elms in the entire country, as well as the North Woods, a remote overgrown forest between 102nd and 106th streets. Past the narrow beauty of Riverside Park on the Upper West Side and the fragrant herb gardens of the Cloisters in Washington Heights' Fort Tryon Park, is Inwood Hill Park, a huge expanse of trees and meadows that's been called one of the most isolated places in Manhattan. Queens is New York's greenest borough, with over half of the city's trees within its borders, including Kissena Park's vintage arboretum and the stately Weeping Beech Tree, a New York City historic landmark.

Above: Central Park in the summer Right: City Hall Park

A City of Saints and Firsts

Everyone in New York likes to think things happen here first. And, of course, they do. New York City can claim America's first 24-hour bank, first algebra book, first automobile accident, first speeding ticket, and the first saint – Mother Cabrini, who came from Italy and now has a shrine in Washington Heights, above Harlem. The first saint born in America was Elizabeth Ann Seton, who hailed from Lower Manhattan and later converted to Catholicism in Little Italy's Old St Patrick's Cathedral.

The first flea circus ("an extraordinary exhibition of industrious fleas") held its opening night at 187 Broadway in January 1835. The first elephant to step ashore in the New World landed here on April 13, 1796. Now the city's exotic wildlife includes the elephants that march through the Queens Midtown Tunnel when the Ringling Brothers Circus comes to town; the alligators that persistent folklorists claim roam the city's sewers (untrue, it seems); and a mysterious colony of ants that was spotted on top of the Empire State Building, nearly 1,500 feet (457 meters) above street level. No one knows how the ants got there, much less why.

A–Z OF NEW YORK

American Museum of Natural History

Guarded by an equestrian statue of Theodore Roosevelt, the museum's main entrance is one of the many additions built around the original structure, a stately Romanesque arcade with two ornate towers, built in 1892. There are 40 exhibition halls housed in 23 buildings. Highlights include a 34-ton meteorite, the world's largest blue sapphire and a renowned anthropological collection. The dinosaur exhibits, installed in six renovated halls, offer an astounding look at life on earth over many millennia. The world's tallest dinosaur – the 50-ft (15-meter) high Barosaurus – can be found in the Theodore Roosevelt Rotunda, and a linked Hall of Biodiversity has a stunning recreation of an African rainforest. The Center for Earth and Space includes a planetarium, and the museum's Naturemax Theatre projects films on a screen four stories high. Location: Central Park West/79th Street. *www.amnh.org*

Battery Park

At the southern tip of Manhattan, Battery Park is named for the battery of cannons that once stood there; it's a pleasant oasis dotted with benches and war memorials, including an old military fortress, Castle Clinton, originally called the West Battery. It also accommodates the Museum of Jewish Heritage – a Living Memorial to the Holocaust that contains poignant letters, photographs and videotaped testimonies from victims (some donated by Stephen Spielberg after he directed the film *Schindler's List*). *www.batteryparkcity.org*

Left: *big bones at the Museum of Natural History*

Bloomingdale's

Serious shoppers head straight for one of the city's retail queens:
Bloomingdale's at 59th Street – a minor institution that most New
Yorkers could not live without. Style and quality are keynotes at
Bloomies. The shop is almost always crowded – it can be oppres-
sively so during holidays and sale times – but if you only go to one
department store in New York City, this should probably be it.
(Entrances are located on both Third and Lexington avenues.)
www.bloomingdales.com

Broadway

At 40th Street is Broadway "proper", a street synonymous with
theaters and the glitzy world of the Great White Way, as this section between 40th and 53rd streets was referred to after electric
light first made its appearance. Its heyday was the 1920–30s,
when there were over 80 theaters on and around Broadway.
The most famous section was 42nd Street – so famous that theater
owners whose properties were on 41st or 43rd Street had pas-
sageways constructed through entire buildings just to be able

to boast a "42nd Street" address. But in the late 1920s the cinema learned to talk, and Broadway theater began to decline. The Great Depression added to Broadway's woes, turning many of the theaters into burlesque houses.

Yet the New York theater still sells more than 11 million tickets annually, earning upwards of $558 million. In an average season of 35 new productions (compared with more than 100 a century ago), roughly half will be new plays. Of 37 "Broadway" theaters, only a handful are on the Great White Way itself, including the Broadway Theatre, the Palace and the Winter Garden. The rest are on the side streets around Broadway and Times Square, from 41st Street as far north as 65th Street.

Although Broadway may make the headlines, off-Broadway is considered by many to be the true soul of New York theater. Occasionally a playwright who achieves fame will bypass Broadway entirely in favor of a smaller venue. The immediacy of the audience, together with the experimental spirit of "fringe" theater, has its avowed fans. Off-Broadway has traditionally been a cautious producer's way of putting on plays considered unsuitable for the mainstream. Today, it's also a way of mounting a production more cheaply, then transferring it to Broadway proper if it's a hit. *www.broadway.com*

Left: Bloomingdale's **Above:** high steppin' on Broadway

The Bronx

In 1641, a Scandinavian, Jonas Bronck, bought 500 acres (200 hectares) of New World virgin forest from Native Americans. Today there is one place where part of the original hemlock forest remains untouched: the 250-acre (100-hectare) New York Botanical Garden. The Bronx River Gorge, which cuts through 10 acres (4 hectares) of woods, is best reached from its arched stone footbridge. The grandest structure in the grounds is the Enid A. Haupt Conservatory, a veritable crystal palace built in 1901 that includes a central Palm Court and connecting greenhouses.

The 265-acre (107-hectare) Bronx Zoo/Wildlife Conservation Park is the country's largest urban zoo – and shares Bronx Park with the Botanical Gardens. The most decorative way to enter is by crossing Fordham Road to the Paul Rainey Memorial Gate, topped with Art Deco bronze casts of animals. Some of the most popular exhibits include the World of Darkness (nocturnal animals).

South Bronx's best-known landmark is baseball's Yankee Stadium, known as The House That Ruth Built. Actually, the nickname is backwards. This is the house built for Ruth. Its shortened

right field was designed for player Babe Ruth's special home-run record. Other baseball stars associated with the stadium include Lou Gehrig, Micky Mantle and Joe DiMaggio.
www.bronxarts.org

Brooklyn

The 70 sq. miles (180 sq. km) on the southeast tip of Long Island encompass the most populous borough of New York City, Brooklyn. More than 2.3 million people live here, which would make it one of the largest metropolises in the United States if it weren't already part of New York City itself. Its development began in the 1600s and continued steadily until 1883, when the Brooklyn Bridge was built across the East River; it slid into obsolescence not long after, when Brooklyn became part of New York City.

The Brooklyn Museum of Art in Flatbush includes an Egyptian collection considered to be the best outside of Cairo and London. The museum also has a changing array of world-class exhibits, 28 period rooms and an unusual outdoor sculpture garden of New York building ornaments. Next door, at the pastoral 50-acre (20-hectare) Brooklyn Botanic Garden, the Japanese gardens alone are worth a visit.

As rents in Manhattan are now out of reach for many, Brooklyn's popularity is rising. No longer considered a boring

Left: Bronx Zoo **Above:** *Bronx Botanical Gardens*

dormitory suburb for commuters, people now live here out of choice. The townhouses in Brooklyn Heights change hands for over a million dollars, and the Promenade along the East River offers a movie-star view of the Brooklyn Bridge and the Manhattan skyline. Most artists have deserted overpriced and over-rated SoHo and TriBeCa, and now congregate in an area of Brooklyn called "DUMBO"(Down Under the Manhattan Bridge Overpass). *www.brooklynonline.com*

Brooklyn Bridge

The world's first suspension bridge is a masterpiece of engineering; a close-up view from the bridge's pedestrian walkway will show the intricacy of its design. The bridge was constructed between 1869 and 1883 by A.J. Roebling and his son. They pioneered the use of steel wire cable to support the suspension bridge, and the criss-cross network of wire gives the bridge what many call a spider-web effect. It has been, and still is, the inspiration of many artists, who get caught up either in its romantic splendor or in the dynamism of its cubist space.

Carnegie Hall

As every New Yorker knows, there's only one way to get to Carnegie Hall – practice. The joke is about as old as the hall itself, which was built in 1891 by industrialist Andrew Carnegie. Ever

*Above: Brooklyn Bridge **Right:** Tavern on the Green, Central Park*

since Tchaikovsky conducted at the opening gala, Carnegie Hall has attracted the world's finest performers, including Rachmaninov, Toscanini and Frank Sinatra. Location: West 57th/7th Avenue. *www.carnegiehall.org*

Central Park

The heart of New York is Central Park, an oasis of lakes and meadows that, for many New Yorkers, is the spiritual calm at the eye of the urban storm. A commission set up in 1811 to decide Manhattan's architectural future envisaged only four squares of green, but protests forced the purchase in 1856 of a 2½-mile (4-km) long, narrow strip of swampland between Eighth and Fifth avenues and 59th and 110th streets, at a cost of $5.5 million.

Architect Frederick Law Olmsted was determined to make the new park as natural as possible. It took 16 years, more than $14 million, 21,000 barrels of dynamite, and the planting of 17,000 trees and shrubs to turn this wilderness into one of the world's first major public parks. Fellow architect Calvert Vaux contributed a formal mall, fountain and ornamental bridges.

Roughly divided into a north and south end – with a reservoir in the middle – the 843-acre (340-hectare) park has entrances at regular intervals around the periphery. At the northern end is the Conservatory Garden, the park's formal horticultural showcase. (To get there, walk through the elegant Vanderbilt Gate at Fifth Avenue and 105th Street.)

Most visitors tend to stick to the park's southern end, entering through the Maine Memorial at Columbus Circle or Grand Army Plaza. Go past the statue of General Sherman and follow the path to get to the Central Park Wildlife Center, known to locals as the Central Park Zoo. Milkmaids once served fresh milk to city kids in the area known as The Dairy; it now serves as Central Park's Visitor Center, offering maps and directions to places like Strawberry Fields, Yoko Ono's memorial to John Lennon. There are also exhibits on the park's history, and information on walking tours.

Above: *the Bethesda Fountain, Central Park*

To the west, Sheep Meadow is popular with picnickers. There's a carousel with handcarved horses and the Wollman Rink for ice skating in winter. Not far from the Tavern On the Green restaurant, follow paths north to The Mall, Central Park's formal promenade. From Bethesda Fountain there's a wonderful view of The Lake; the Loeb Boathouse has boats and bikes for hire. Northeast, the Ramble is the wild heart of the park. Its twisting paths and rocky cliffs are a favorite with birdwatchers in search of the 250-plus migratory species that stop off here. Despite its reputation, Central Park has one of the city's lowest crime rates, but mugging is not unknown and you shouldn't wander off the paths alone. *www.centralpark.org*

Chelsea

Chelsea has a thriving art gallery scene, a flourishing gay scene along Eighth Avenue, as well as Chelsea Piers, a riverside sports and entertainment development that attracts an estimated 8,000 visitors a day. West of Fifth Avenue to the Hudson River, from 14th up to about 30th Street, Chelsea borders the midtown Garment District and includes the Flower District, wedged between 28th and 30th along the Avenue of the Americas (more usually known as Sixth Avenue). It's a great neighborhood to stroll around, and bars and cafes on almost every street corner can provide brunch, lunch, snacks or dinner.

Right: *clubbers ready to party*

One of Chelsea's most popular shopping sites is the flea market (open weekends) on Sixth between 25th and 27th streets, where you can find anything from antique clothes to jewelry to furniture. *www.chealseapiers.com*

Chelsea Hotel

At 222 West 23rd Street is the gothic-looking Chelsea Hotel, almost half way between Seventh and Eighth avenues. One of the city's most famous residential hotels, the list of artists who've lived here since 1909 includes Thomas Wolfe, Arthur Miller, Jack Kerouac, Brendan Behan and Virgil Thompson. This is where Andy Warhol filmed *Chelsea Girls* in 1967 and also where punk-rocker Sid Vicious murdered his girlfriend before dying of a drug overdose several weeks later. *www.hotelchelsea.com*

Above: *gossiping in Chinatown*

Chinatown

The telephone booths have pagoda roofs, shop signs are written in Chinese, shopkeepers can be seen carrying crates of exotic vegetables and red ducks dangle from shop windows. Begun in the 1870s, the neighborhood is now one of the largest Chinese-American communities in the US. It has been estimated that this section of the city is home to about 150,000 people, and growing, with most residents coming from Taiwan and Hong Kong.

A good way to learn more is to stop by the Museum of Chinese in the Americas. Founded in 1970, it features a permanent exhibit covering the Chinese-American experience, and it also organizes various walking tours and lectures. New Yorkers flock to Chinatown on Sundays for *dim sum* brunches, and during the rest of the week to eat in one of any number of excellent, unpretentious restaurants. *www.nychinatown.com*

Chrysler Building

The Chrysler Building is one of the jewels of the Manhattan skyline, lifting the spirit every time it looms into view. Designed in secret by William Van Alen and erected by auto czar Walter Chrysler in 1930, its distinctive Art Deco spire rises nearly 1,000 feet (300 meters) into the air like a stainless-steel rocket ship. Stop in to admire the lobby's marble-and-bronze decor, enhanced by epic murals depicting transportation and human endeavor. Location: Lexington/East 42nd Street.

Right: *the Chrysler Building*

The Cloisters

The Uptown branch of the Metropolitan Museum of Art, the Cloisters is worth a trip to Washington Heights in the far northern edges of Manhattan. Imported from Europe and reassembled here, stone by stone, are French and Spanish monastic cloisters; a 12th-century chapter house; the Fuentaduena Chapel and both a Gothic and a Romanesque chapel. The prize of this medieval collection is the Unicorn Tapestries – six handwoven cloths from the 15th century. *www.metmuseum.org*

Coney Island

On the coast to the south of Brooklyn lies Coney Island, which is actually a peninsula. The Aquarium for Wildlife Conservation, more familiarly known as the New York Aquarium, is located at West 8th Street and Surf Avenue. Overhauled not long ago, with an outdoor theater for sea lion performances, this metropolitan home for ocean life is one of Brooklyn's most popular attractions.

New Yorkers have been escaping to Coney Island since the 1840s and in greater numbers after 1875, when the train connected the beach with the city. Today it retains a faded, dated "kitsch" feel beloved by some purists. You can still tempt fate and hang on for dear life aboard the Cyclone, with its wooden track and speeding cars. And you can still walk along the boardwalk watching seagulls.

Farther east on the boardwalk is Brighton Beach, which for

*Above: window in the Cloisters **Right:** Coney Island thriller*

many years was an enclave of elderly Jews and made famous by playwright Neil Simon. In the mid-1970s, a wave of immigrants, mostly Russians and Ukrainians, began moving into Brighton Beach, which soon became known as "Little Odessa." *www.coneyislandusa.com*

Ellis Island

This island is now a museum dedicated to its original purpose as the main gateway to the US for the millions of immigrants between 1892 and 1924, and exhibits delve into the stories of those who passed through it. Life was hard: laws barred the sick, the weak, the politically undesirable, the penniless, and even unmarried women from entering the "land of the free". Two thousand immigrants a day was no rarity in the record years of 1907 and 1914, and conditions in the Great Hall were appalling. A visit here is a sobering experience, but should not be missed. Restoration work was completed on the buildings in 1990. *www.ellisisland.org*

Empire State Building

The building, the world's highest when completed in 1931, rises like a rocket from the corner of Fifth Avenue and 34th Street. On a clear day you can see as far as 80 miles (128km). Take the elevator to the 86th-floor observation deck; a second elevator goes from here up to the tiny lookout on the 102nd floor, which is just about where Fay Wray had her fateful rendezvous with a 50-ft (15-meter) ape by the name of King Kong. A great time to visit is late afternoon, to catch both daytime and evening views: Manhattan by day is remarkable; by night memorable. One of the easiest buildings to identify on the Manhattan skyline is the famed Chrysler Building. On the second floor of the Empire State Building, the New York Skyride offers a dizzying simulated flight through the city.

www.esbnyc.com

Flatiron Building

The triangular Flatiron Building, 285 feet (87 meters) high, raised eyebrows and hopes for a bright future when it was erected in 1902. Now it serves as the unofficial gateway to "Downtown New York." Although originally known as the Fuller Building, the skyscraper was soon dubbed the Flatiron because of its distinctive shape. Location: Broadway/E. 21st Street

Frick Collection

This collection of art treasures, assembled by steel manufacturer Henry Clay Frick, and housed in his former palazzo, was built in French Neo-Classical

Left: the Flatiron Building

style in 1913. Efforts have been made to keep it more of a house and less of a museum. Goya, Titian, El Greco, Vermeer and Renoir are just a few of the artists who are represented here. Location: Fifth Avenue and 70th Street. *www.frick.org*

Grand Central

Grand Central is the hub in a spoke of Metro-North commuter lines reaching deep into the suburbs of Westchester County and neighboring Connecticut, and it is used by almost half a million passengers each day, on over 550 trains. Unlike the old Pennsylvania Station, Grand Central was saved from demolition by the city's Landmarks Preservation Commission, and thus this 1913 Beaux Arts reminder of a bygone era, when travel was a gracious experience, remains almost intact. It has undergone a $200 million restoration to renew its former glory – the glorious illuminated zodiac on the vaulted ceiling of the main concourse – one of the world's largest rooms – gleams like new.

Greenwich Village

"The Village" is more about ambiance than landmarks; here you can find cobblestone alleys, graceful architecture, Italian bakeries, gourmet markets, theaters and the oldest gay community in New York. Christopher Street is the symbolic center

Above: *Grand Central's famous Oyster Bar*

of the gay community. In addition, there's a remarkable array of restaurants, bars, and jazz clubs. Bordered by 14th Street to the north, the Hudson River to the west and Broadway to the east, it's where the offbeat is the norm, and where the annual Halloween Parade has to be one of the world's best spectacles.

Two of the most picturesque streets in the city are 9th and 10th; lined by stately brick and brownstone houses, these desirable residential byways have been home to numerous artists and writers (Mark Twain lived at 14 West 10th).

As in other Manhattan areas, real estate prices have forced out all but the most affluent, but the Village is still where many people would prefer to live. The corner of Bleecker and Macdougal, once beatnik heaven, is a good place to soak up the Village feeling, although these days it tends to be a magnet for out-of-towners, who are drawn by the bevy of ersatz crafts shops and "authentic" ethnic eateries. Bibliophiles will be overwhelmed by the Strand Bookstore (Broadway/12th Street), which claims to have eight miles of used books.
www.greenwich-village.com

Guggenheim Museum

Located at 1071 Fifth Avenue at the corner of 88th Street, the white funnel-shaped structure of the Solomon R. Guggenheim Museum, resembling an upturned snail-shell, has been the source of debate since it opened in 1959. Some say that Frank Lloyd Wright's design, 16 years in the making, is an architectural masterpiece. Others think it's more akin to a parking garage than an art gallery and definitely out of place next to the handsome townhouses that give the Upper East Side its special charm.

Whatever your opinion, take the elevator to the top floor and slowly make your way down the spiral ramp. Although exhibitions change frequently, they are likely to include works by Renoir, Manet, Chagall, Degas, van Gogh, Toulouse-Lautrec, Gauguin, Kandinsky, Klee and Picasso. All in all, not a bad crowd. A newer building – which rather dominates the original – was opened in 1992 to provide more space for the huge collection of over 4,000 paintings, sculptures, and drawings. *www.guggenheim.org*

Harlem

Geographically there is an East Harlem (Madison Avenue to the East River, sometimes called Spanish Harlem), its residents by and large having close ties with Puerto Rico; a Central Harlem (Fifth Avenue to St Nicholas Avenue), whose citizens are over-

Left: pigs fly in Greenwich Village **Above:** *the Guggenheim Museum*

whelmingly African-American; and a West Harlem, which extends to Riverside Drive. In general, West Harlem has a larger population of white residents than the others and includes the neighborhoods of Morningside Heights and Hamilton Heights. Farther up, Washington Heights is close to Manhattan's northern tip, and is an ethnically mixed area with cultural treasures.

Originally named for Haarlem in the Netherlands, New York City's first upscale suburb was made more accessible with the opening of the Harlem River Railroad, the extension of the rapid transit lines in 1880, and in 1904 by the building of the IRT Lenox Avenue subway. There followed an influx of immigrants and, from the early 1900s, Harlem became an African-American enclave. Today it is a diverse community where Irish, Italian, Dominican, Haitian, Puerto Rican, West African and other residents sometimes live side by side, and where ongoing renovations are attracting increasing numbers of middle-class African-American and white professionals and artists. Nevertheless, there are some areas tourists should avoid. To best experience this part of the city, take a tour or contact the Harlem Visitors and Convention Association.

The neighborhood around 125th Street is the best place for annual events that highlight Harlem's cultural richness. These include the Black World Championship Rodeo, held every spring,

Above: *doing the Harlem shuffle*

which brings the role of African-Americans in the history of the American West to wider public attention; the Jazzmobile concerts, presented outdoors throughout the summer; and the African-American Day Parade, held in early September. The largest annual event is Harlem Week, which is held during the first three weeks of August. With a multitude of cultural activities taking place throughout the neighborhood, Harlem Week claims it is the third-largest summer festival in the country.

Lincoln Center for the Performing Arts

Construction on the center began in 1959 as part of a massive redevelopment plan intended to clean up the slum that used to occupy the site. More than 180 buildings were demolished and 1,600 families relocated in order to make room for the complex, inflaming social critics who saw it as nothing more than a playground for the elite. Today the center sells about 5 million tickets a year. Standing at the black marble fountain in the middle of the plaza – a computer links the fountain to wind velocity so that people do not get hit by the spray – you are surrounded by the glass and white marble facades of the center's three main structures.

The Metropolitan Opera is directly in front with two large murals by Marc Chagall hanging behind the glass wall – *Le Triomphe de la Musique* to the left, *Les Sources de la Musique* to the right. The Met is home to the Metropolitan Opera Company from September to April and the American Ballet Theater from May to July.

Right: Lincoln Center

To the left of the central fountain, the New York State Theater is shared by the New York City Opera and the New York City Ballet. If the doors are open, look at the Jasper Johns painting on the ground floor and the two controversial marble statues by Elie Nadelman in the upstairs foyer.

The third side of the main plaza is occupied by Avery Fisher Hall, home of the New York Philharmonic and the Mostly Mozart series held in the summer. It's worth peeking inside for a look at Richard Lippold's *Orpheus and Apollo*, a hanging metal sculpture that dominates the foyer.
www.lincolncenter.org

Little Italy

One of Manhattan's smallest and most tradition-bound neighborhoods, wedged between Chinatown and SoHo, Little Italy has been an Italian enclave since the late 1800s when large waves of immigrants arrived in New York from Southern Europe. The most pleasant strip is along Mulberry Street, north of Canal, where the atmosphere abruptly changes from boisterous to

almost mellow, and the sidewalks are lined by cafes and social clubs rather than clamorous street vendors.
www.littleitalynyc.com

Lower East Side

The tenement capital of New York City, where only a few modern freestanding highrises have altered the landscape from how it has been for the past 100 years, the Lower East Side was a center for the early garment industry in New York. The poor, mainly Jewish immigrants who settled here worked long hours for slave wages under terrible conditions. Today, the Lower East Side Tenement Museum, at 90 Orchard Street, is a testament to that struggle. The old Bowery Bank building at 124 Bowery is a landmark, with its interior one of the grandest spaces in New York.

Macy's

At Herald Square stands Macy's, which claims to be the biggest department store in the world. Stroll across the ground floor just to take in the huge selection of goods. Macy's was built on the site of the former Metropolitan Opera House, which moved to the Lincoln Center in 1966.
www.macys.com

Left: *residents of Little Italy* **Above:** *Hebrew sign, Lower East Side*

Metropolitan Museum of Art

Located on 82nd Street, this is the largest art museum in the US and one of the world's most impressive centers of culture. In a maze of galleries, gardens and period rooms within a sprawling Gothic giant built in stages from 1874, it houses a vast treasure trove of art in over a dozen distinct collections, along with a regular series of spectacular special exhibitions.

The Met's "must sees" include the American Wing, which contains one of the best collections of American art in the world; the Robert Lehman Collection (European art including works by Rembrandt, Goya, Van Gogh and Matisse); Drawings, Prints, and Photographs (artists represented include Leonardo da Vinci, Titian, Michelangelo, Turner, and Degas); and the magnificent Egyptian Collection's reconstructed Temple of Dendur.

Native American and Pacific Island art can be admired in the Michael C. Rockefeller wing, and the Islamic, Greco-Roman, and Asian art collections are truly spectacular. A recent addition

Above: the Metropolitan Museum of Art

is the Lila Acheson Wallace Wing (1987), and there is a roof-garden with a superb view of Central Park.
www.metmuseum.org

The Museum of Modern Art

MOMA, on 11 W 53rd Street, is considered by many to be the most important museum of modern art in the world, with exhibits by Van Gogh, Monet, Matisse, Toulouse-Lautrec and Picasso. There is also an architecture and design section, with works by Tiffany, Thonet and Marcel Breuer, as well as a fine photography section. In the midst of this awe-inspiring art is the wonderful Sculpture Garden, designed by Philip Johnson.

The museum was founded by Abby Rockefeller, the wife of John D Rockefeller Jr., a passionate collector of modern art.

Opened in 1929, the collection was shifted to its present home 10 years later. In 1951, architect Philip Johnson added two wings; during the 1960s several neighboring buildings were acquired; and in 1983 the western part of the building was provided with a controversial 42-story apartment tower that doubled the museum's exhibition space, providing expansive room for Cubists, Expressionists, Pop Artists and Dadaists.

Exhibition space is currently being doubled again, absorbing an adjacent hotel, and is due for completion by 2004.
www.moma.org

Above: MOMA's fabulous gift shop

The Museum of Television and Radio

The perfect place for couch potatoes and students of Americana, this museum (25 West 52nd Street) founded by TV magnate William S. Paley is also a valuable resource for media buffs, comprising gallery space, two theaters, and a screening room that shows retrospectives of great directors. It's main appeal, however, is a vast archive of vintage radio and TV programs that can be rented for an hour at a time. The museum is perfect for rainy-day activities, except for Mondays, when it's closed. *www.mtr.org*

New York Public Library

An unlikely mix of office workers, layabouts and footsore tourists can usually be found lounging on the stairway under the gaze of "Patience" and "Fortitude," the two marble lions reclining on the top steps of the library. Located at the corner of 42nd Street, this Beaux Arts monument, built in 1911, now houses one of the finest research facilities in the world with some 88 miles (140 km) of bookshelves and an archive collection that includes the first book printed in the US, the *Bay Psalm Book* from 1640, and the original diaries of Virginia Woolf.

The biggest treasure of all, however, may be the restored reading room, a vast, gilded gem where the windows overlook adjacent Bryant Park. Ask inside about joining one of the twice-daily tours of the enormous building.
www.nypl.org

Left: a lion outside the library

Plaza Hotel

New York hotels come and go, but the Plaza reigns supreme. This 19th-century mansion at Grand Army Plaza overlooking Central Park has been the home away from home to Mark Twain, Frank Lloyd Wright and several presidents. Modern-day celebrities still favor its old-world charm and discreet security: Liz Taylor and Richard Burton stayed here at the height of their fame, and Michael Douglas and Catherine Zeta-Jones tied the knot at the Plaza in 2000. *www.plaza-athenee.com*

Queens

Every visitor who lands at JFK International Airport and takes a taxi to Manhattan goes through the borough of Queens (named for Queen Catherine of Braganza, wife of Charles II of England). This is one of the world's most diverse communities, with one of the largest Greek neighborhoods outside of Athens and areas filled with immigrants from India, Pakistan, Thailand, South America and Europe.

Above: *an alternative to the yellow cabs*

It contains relics of the 1939 and 1964 World Fairs, and such sporty attractions as the USTA National Tennis Center, the site of the annual US Open, and Shea Stadium, the Mets' home, just beyond the subway station, with its capacity to seat 55,000 cheering baseball fans.
www.queens.about.com

Radio City Music Hall

One of the highlights of Rockefeller Center is the Art Deco Radio City Music Hall on Sixth Avenue. Built during the Great Depression – it was opened in 1932 – the sheer amount of pomp and splendor inside is surprising for that era. The six-story foyer contains a magnificent staircase, the seats are upholstered in velvet, and the stage is as wide as a city block. The satin curtain weighs 3 tons and is raised and lowered by 13 motors. The sun, moon, and stars appear at the touch of a button; likewise lightning and storm effects. The enormous 6,200-seat auditorium was always sold out, even during the Depression, when the theater either presented the famous Rockettes revue group, or the very latest movies on a huge screen. As television hit theater attendances, rumors of demolition were rife, but New Yorkers amassed a small fortune to save their last great entertainment center, and Radio City underwent restoration. Today it is a landmark building, and hosts extravagant shows as well as popular-music concerts. A guided tour is worthwhile.
www.radiocity.com

Above: *Art Deco Radio City* ***Right:*** *Rockefeller Center*

Rockefeller Center

At 49th Street, Fifth Avenue really begins to live up to its legend as the playground of New York's wealthiest families, thanks to Rockefeller Center, the world's largest privately owned business and entertainment complex and an absolute triumph of Art Deco architecture. This huge compound of office towers is a "city within the city," and extends from Fifth to beyond Sixth Avenue and from 48th to north of 51st Street.

The entire compound was financed by just one man: John D Rockefeller, Jr. The Rockefeller name is synonymous with wealth, but the surprising thing about the center is that John D. managed to come up with the $125 million needed for its construction during the Great Depression. The first 14 buildings were constructed between 1931 and 1940. Thousands of people who would otherwise have remained unemployed found work here.

The Channel Gardens – so named because they separate La Maison Française on the left and the British Building on the right – draw visitors to the centerpiece of the complex, the Sunken Plaza, which serves as a skating rink in winter and an outdoor cafe in summer.

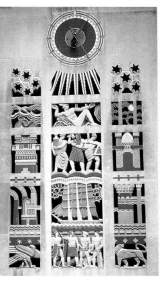

Colorful flags flap, and an 18-ft (5-meter) gilded statue of Prometheus, the work of Paul Manship, hovers in front of the waterfall by the soaring General Electric building.

There are more than 100 paintings and sculptures by more than 30 artists within the complex. Outside the International Building on Fifth Avenue is Lee Lawrie's *Atlas*; another work by the same artist, *Wisdom*, can be seen above the entrance portal of the General Electric (formerly RCA) building. Lee Lawrie's striking stone relief, *Genius*, looms over the entrance; inside, the main lobby features two murals by José María Sert, American *Progress* and *Time*.

The lobby information desk can give details about taking one of the NBC Studio tours offered regularly throughout the day. *www.rockefellercenter.com*

Russian Tea Room

Founded by members of the Russian Corps de Ballet, over the years the Tea Room has attracted its share of Broadway stars and Hollywood luminaries. Formal, elegant and *the* place for tea (or vodka), it's recently been renovated to its former glory. Location: West 57th between Sixth and Seventh Avenues. *web.russiantearoom.com*

Above: detail from the International Building, Rockefeller Center

Saks Fifth Avenue

One of the city's finest department stores is across the street from Rockefeller Center. The super-rich (and those who like to pretend) can be seen bouncing between Cartier, Fortunoff, Bijan and Gucci between 52nd and 54th streets, to name a few of the high-class boutiques that give the area its panache.
www.saksfifthavenue.com

SoHo

Once New York City's most fashionable shopping and hotel district, by the end of the 19th century the narrow streets of SoHo were filled by factories whose cast-iron facades masked sweatshop conditions so horrific that the city fire department dubbed the area "Hell's Hundred Acres". The entire area might have been razed in the 1960s if local artists hadn't started moving into the old lofts. Today only the most successful artists can afford to live here.

In the late 19th century, Greene Street was the center of New York's most notorious red-light district; nowadays it offers a rich concentration of uniquely American architecture, including (at the Canal Street end) the city's longest continuous row of cast-iron buildings. For art lovers, there are plenty of contemporary galleries to look around.
www.artseensoho.com

South Street Seaport Museum

It's not really a museum so much as an enclave of historic buildings converted into a trendy market-place à la Boston's Quincy Market

Right: SoHo sculpture

or London's Covent Garden. After years of neglect, the area was rediscovered by commercial developers, and before New Yorkers knew what hit them, another desirable area was born. The 19th-century buildings that once housed shipping firms and sailmakers are now occupied by boutiques, cafes and restaurants. About the only thing that hasn't changed is the old Fulton Fish Market. It's still the city's busiest fish wholesaler, and is open every weeknight from midnight to about 8am. The Seaport is spacious, quaint, friendly, clean, and a heck of a lot slower than the rest of New York. The cobblestone streets are made for strolling, and the shops are great for browsing.
www.southstseaport.org

St Patrick's Cathedral

Opened in 1879, St. Patrick's is the country's largest Catholic church and now one of Midtown's most formidable landmarks; its ornate

Gothic facade counterpoints against the angular lines and smooth surfaces of the skyscrapers around it. And yet St Pat's is unmistakably New York: where else would you need tickets to attend Midnight Mass? Take some time for a look round the cathedral's magnificent interior; the bronze doors and stained-glass windows are particularly striking.
www.oldsaintpatricks.org

Above: St Patrick's Cathedral is the country's largest Catholic church

Staten Island

The second-smallest and least-known borough is to many only the island where the famous ferry goes: the excursion from South Ferry (next to Battery Park in Manhattan) includes a view of the Statue of Liberty and the Manhattan skyline, and runs well into the evening. But it is worth disembarking on Staten Island itself. The ferry lands in the town of St George, where nearby attractions include the Staten Island Institute of Arts & Sciences, with local historical exhibits.

Snug Harbor Cultural Center opened in 1831 as Sailors' Snug Harbor, a home for retired seamen. Now its 83 acres (34 hectares) of ponds, wetlands and woodlands are a haven for nature and the arts. The main buildings are Greek Revival landmarks: Neptune, tridents, parrots and ships still decorate the Main Hall interior, just as they did when the building served as quarters for the old sailors. Today, the Newhouse Center for Contemporary Art features works by emerging and mid-career artists in all media.

Above: the ferry to Staten Island offers great views

Outside, close to the pretty and romantic old gazebo, Snug Harbor holds an impressive range of concerts and performances. Other parts of Staten Island's renovation include the Veterans' Memorial Hall and an 1892 Music Hall. Also on the grounds is the Staten Island Botanical Garden, noted for its orchid collection and Chinese Scholar's Garden; and the Staten Island Children's Museum, another excellent interactive experience. *www.silive.com*

The Statue of Liberty

Since it was dedicated in 1886, the Statue of Liberty, 151 ft (46 meters) high with a pedestal nearly the same height, has welcomed millions of immigrants into New York Harbor. The statue is itself an immigrant, having been a gift to the US from France. It attracts well over a million tourists a year. The big attraction is climbing to the top – a grueling challenge, especially since there's no air conditioning. For a quicker glimpse of the statue, hop on board the famous Staten Island Ferry *(see above)*. *www.libertystatepark.com*

Tiffany and Co.

Designer-street East 57th kicks off with the world-famous jewelry and glassware store. The main object of admiration is the Tiffany diamond, one of the biggest yellow diamonds – 128.54 carats when cut – ever found. Its 90 facets (32 more than the standard brilliant cut) reflect the light like the dancing flames of a fire.

www.tiffany.com

Times Square

Named for the *New York Times* newspaper, which moved into offices here in 1904, this square at the junction of Broadway and Seventh Avenue is at the heart of the entertainment district. During the Golden Age of the Theater District in the 1920s, big-name producers staged as many as 250 shows a year in the area. That same decade, Prohibition brought speakeasies, gangsters and Damon Runyon stories to the square.

Times Square is also the site of the city's boisterous annual New Year's Eve celebration. These days, more than 35 Broadway theaters attract audiences to over 30 new theatrical productions a year. Several vintage theaters in the area have recently been saved, and then renovated, and after a long period of decline the refurbished Times Square is again one of the city's most popular tourist destinations.

www.timessquarebid.org

Left: Liberty mementos **Above:** New York's finest, plus friend

TriBeCa

In the late 1970s, artists in search of cheaper rents migrated south from SoHo to TriBeCa – the Triangle Below Canal – which lies south of Canal Street to Chambers Street, and west from Broadway to the Hudson River. Called Washington Market in the days when the city's major produce businesses operated here (before they moved to Hunt's Point in the Bronx), this part of the Lower West Side is one of Manhattan's best neighborhoods for stolling around and taking in the scene.

An eclectic blend of renovated warehouses that sport Corinthian columns, condominium towers and celebrity restaurants, TriBeCa's somewhat residential atmosphere is a pleasant change of pace from SoHo's tourist-packed streets. Greenwich Street is where much of TriBeCa's new development is centered, although you can still find some authentic early remnants, like the 19th-century lantern factory between Laight and Vestry streets that are now million-dollar lofts.

Above: *artists in search of cheaper rents put TriBeCa on the map*

Trump Tower

Fifth Avenue's glitz is epitomized by this building between 56th and 57th streets. The design, with its cool marble and a five-story waterfall, may be a little overdone, but it's effective. The 68-story complex includes restaurants, stores and pricey condominium apartments. Most shops are also beyond many people's budgets, but window-shopping is free.
www.trumpworldtower.com

Union Square

Named for the convergence of Broadway and Fourth Avenue, Union Square sits between 17th and 14th streets. A stylish prospect in the mid-1850s, by the turn of the 20th century it was more or less deserted by residents and became a thriving theater center. Today, Union Square bustles with life, a resurgence that might be attributed to the Greenmarket, which brings farmers and their produce to the northern edge of the square four days a week. It's a great place to wander around on a Saturday morning.

United Nations

For a fascinating look at the workings of international diplomacy, don't miss the UN on 46th Street and First Avenue. Free tickets are available for meetings of the General Assembly when it's in session. Don't miss the moon rock display just inside the entrance, the Marc Chagall stained-glass windows, or the gift shop, which sells

Right: *sculpture in front of the United Nations building*

handicrafts from all over the world. On weekdays, you can have lunch in the Delegates' Dining Room, where the view of the river is almost as interesting as the myriad opportunities for multi-lingual eavesdropping. *www.un.org*

Upper West Side

The apartments overlooking Central Park are among the most lavish in the city, and the cross streets, especially 74th, 75th and 76th, are lined with splendid brownstones.

The most famous building on this stretch is The Dakota (1 West 72nd Street), built in 1884 by Henry Hardenbergh. It has attracted tenants like Boris Karloff, Leonard Bernstein, Lauren Bacall and John Lennon, who was shot outside in 1980.

US Custom House

Located across from the Bowling Green subway station in downtown Manhattan, this former custom house was designed by Cass Gilbert and built in 1907. A magnificent example of Beaux-Arts architecture, the facade is embellished by ornate limestone sculptures that represent the four continents and "eight races" of mankind. Inside is the (free) George Gustave Heye Center of the National Museum of the American Indian, with exhibits that range from priceless Navaho rugs to mini-histories of Mayan textiles. An underrated New York museum.

Above: the Upper West Side **Right:** *Wall Street trading floor*

Wall Street

Viewed from the outside, the New York Stock Exchange looks like a temple, with its huge pillars and elaborate frieze on the portico. It was built in 1903 and enlarged in 1923. At the Visitor Center, guards direct visitors to a gallery overlooking the main floor. Here, a number of interactive machines and displays shed some light on the feverish activities of the folks downstairs. The sign-language used by today's brokers is supposed to date back to the time when partners in adjoining buildings had to be informed about buying and selling from the sidewalk below.

Washington Square

The geographical and spiritual heart of Greenwich Village, Washington Square is where all of New York comes to play. On a warm day you can see serious chess masters, amateur musicians, boisterous students and young mothers relaxing on the grass, or taking a stroll. The centerpiece is the Washington Arch, first designed in 1889, then replaced by the imposing marble version in 1918. *www.washingtonsquarepark.org*

Whitney Museum of American Art

The Whitney Museum is set among the glossy array of boutiques and galleries along Madison Avenue. Marcel Breuer's cantilevered structure is a work of art in its own right, and it stands alongside the Guggenheim as one of the Upper East Side's boldest architectural statements.

Founded in 1930 by Gertrude Vanderbilt Whitney, a wealthy sculptor who helped young artists to exhibit their work in Greenwich Village as early as the 1930s, the Whitney since then has made a policy of acquiring pieces that represent the full range of 20th-century American art, including the works of Georgia O'Keeffe, Willem de Kooning and Jasper Johns. "Classics" in its collection include Lichtenstein, Pollock, Rauschenberg, and Shan. One highlight not to be missed is the 2,000 or so works by Edward Hopper.

www.whitney.org

Above: *Zabar's food shop is the best in town*

World Trade Center

Rising a plucky 110 stories, the World Trade Center remains New York's biggest tourist attraction. An estimated 1.8 million visitors flock to the Trade Center's famous Twin Towers every year, which are the best-known structures in a 16-acre (6-hectare), seven-building complex that took 17 years, 200,000 tons of steel and 425,000 cubic yards (325,000 cubic meters) of cement to build.

The elevator ride up to the South Tower's 107th-floor Observation Deck (Two World Trade Center) is a stomach-dropping, ear-popping experience. The Top of the World Observation Deck on the 107th floor will give you your best view of Downtown Manhattan and the islands in the mouth of the Hudson River. There's an even more spectacular vista from the open-air rooftop promenade, 1,377 feet (420 meters) above sea level on the 110th floor.

www.wtc-top.com

Zabar's

Zabar's is the gourmet food shop against which all gourmet shops are measured. Even if you have no intention of buying, you can elbow your way through the crowds to the counter for free samples of the best hams, cheeses, patés and olives in the city. If you walked in on a full stomach, you're guaranteed to walk out hungry again. Location: West 80th/Broadway. *www.zabars.co*

Right: World Trade Center

ESSENTIAL INFORMATION

The Place

New York City lies in the southeast corner of New York state at the mouth of the Hudson River. It covers about 300 sq. miles (780 sq. km.) Greater New York is divided into five boroughs: Manhattan, the Bronx, Queens, Brooklyn and Staten Island. Manhattan is the smallest but most densely populated.

Population: 7,342,636 (Federal Census Bureau, 1998).

Time Zone: Eastern Standard Time (EST); five hours behind London; one hour ahead of Chicago; three hours ahead of LA.

Currency: US dollars and cents.

Weights and Measures: The US uses the Imperial system; metric weights and measures are rarely used.

Electricity: 110 volts.

Local Dialing Codes: Manhattan is 212 and the newer 646. Brooklyn, Staten Island, Queens, and the Bronx are 718 and the newer 347. Unless otherwise stated, the numbers in this book are the 212 code.

The Climate

New York has four distinct seasons, and is generally at its best during the spring and fall months. Summer temperatures hover in the mid-70 to mid-80°F (24–29°C), although heatwaves where the mercury rises to 100°F (37.8°C) may occur and uncomfortable humidity is often the rule, especially in July and August. September and October sometimes usher in a balmy, dry "Indian summer." Winter temperatures can be 10 or 15°F (-12 or -9°C), with the average temperature for January closer to 32° F (0°C).

Left: view from the Empire State Building

The Economy

New York City is the world's foremost financial center (the New York Stock Exchange, Federal Reserve Bank, commodities exchanges, etc. are all located here.) It holds a leading position in the retail and wholesale trades, manufacturing, fashion, art and the service industries. New York is also a major center for media, with new-media companies that develop interactive software and on-line computer services an increasingly important segment of the industry.

Public Holidays and Festivals

As with other countries in the world, the US has gradually shifted most of its public holidays to the Monday closest to the actual dates, creating a number of three-day weekends throughout the year. Holidays that are celebrated no matter what day on which they fall are: New Year's Day (January 1); Independence Day (July 4); Veterans' Day (November 11); Christmas Day (December 25).

Other holidays are: Martin Luther King Jr Day (third Mon in Jan); President's Day (third Mon in Feb); Memorial Day (last Mon in May); Labor Day (first Mon in Sept); Columbus Day (second Mon in Oct); Thanksgiving (fourth Thurs in November).

New York has festivals throughout the year, but highlights include Harlem Week (Aug); the Feast of San Gennaro, Little Italy (Sept); and rip-roaring parades down Fifth Avenue on St Patrick's Day and at Easter.

Left: Fourth of July store design

Getting There

BY AIR

East of Manhattan on Long Island, New York's two major airports, John F. Kennedy International and LaGuardia, are respectively 15 and 8 miles (24 km and 13 km) from the city, with driving time from Kennedy estimated at just under one hour. In practice, heavy traffic can sometimes double this. Most charters and domestic flights and some international flights use LaGuardia. New York's third airport, Newark, is in New Jersey and, although further away from Manhattan than JFK and LaGuardia, can be easier to arrive in, and buses into town are frequent.

BY SEA

Stretching along the Hudson River from 48th to 52nd streets in Manhattan, the Passenger Ship Terminal, tel: 246 5450, at Piers 88, 90 and 92, has customs facilities, baggage handling, rooftop parking and bus connections to the Midtown area.

BY RAIL

Trains arrive and depart from Manhattan's two railroad terminals: Grand Central at Park Avenue and 42nd Street, and Penn Station at Seventh Avenue and 33rd Street. City buses stop outside each terminal and each sits atop a subway station. Amtrak information, tel: 582 6875, or (toll-free) 1-800-872 7245.

Above: Grand Central timepiece

BY ROAD

Driving in from the Long Island airports, access is via the Midtown Tunnel or across the Triborough Bridge and down Manhattan's East River Drive. The city's main bus terminal, the Port Authority (Eighth Ave between 40th and 42nd Street), sits atop two subway lines and is serviced by long distance bus companies (including Greyhound) as well as local commuter lines. City buses stop outside. A modern terminal with shops and facilities, it tends to attract its share of riff-raff; although well-policed, it's not the sort of place to leave bags unguarded.

Entry Regulations

A passport, a photograph, a visitor's visa, proof of intent to leave after your visit and, depending upon your country of origin, an international vaccination certificate, are required of most foreign nationals for entry into the US. Visitors from many European countries staying less than 90 days no longer need a visa.

Above: the only way to travel

Health

Medical services in the US are among the most expensive in the world. Always travel with full and comprehensive travel insurance to cover any emergencies.

Money

Credit cards are accepted almost everywhere, although not all cards at all places. Along with out-of-state or overseas bank cards, they can also be used to withdraw money at ATMs (automatic teller machines), but a fee is usually charged. Dollar traveler's checks are accepted in most hotels and good restaurants, so long as they are accompanied by proper identification.

Security and Crime

Despite its history as a hotbed of crime, a recent FBI report says that New York has the lowest crime rate of any of the US's top 25 cities. It pays to remain alert, however, and the rules of the urban jungle apply: lock valuables in the hotel safe, lock your hotel door while inside, conceal expensive cameras while on the street, avoid parks and deserted streets after dark.

Tipping

Many New Yorkers rely on tips to make up for what are often poor hourly salaries. Unless service is truly horrendous, you can figure on tipping everyone from bellmen and porters to hotel doormen and maids. In restaurants, the easiest way to figure out the amount

Right: the seal of the boys in blue

for the tip is to double the tax; in taxis, tip as much as 15 percent of the total fare, with a 50¢ minimum.

Useful Addresses

● The New York Convention & Visitors Bureau, 810 Seventh Ave, New York, NY 10019, tel: 212-397 8222; 1-800-NYCVISIT; www.nycvisit.com, has maps and information about hotel packages and discount admission programs. They also publish the Official NYC Guide, a comprehensive listing of activities, hotels, tours, restaurants, etc. Walk-in visitors are welcome at the NYCVB's Visitor Information Center, tel: 484 1222, same address as above, located between 52nd and 53rd streets.

● The Times Square Visitors Center at the Embassy Theater, 1560 Broadway between 46th and 47th streets is another good source of information, and features a ticket center for Broadway shows, as well as useful facilities like e-mail and currency exchange counters.

● The Harlem Visitors & Convention Association, 219 West 135th St, New York, NY 10030, tel: 212-862 8497; fax: 862 8745. An essential source of information about Harlem.

● The Bronx Council on the Arts, 1738 Hone Ave, Bronx NY 10461, tel: 718-931 9500. Offers information about art, music and other events.

Above: maps are available from the Visitors Bureau

● The Brooklyn Tourism Council, 30 Flatbush Ave, Brooklyn, NY 11217, tel: 718-855 7882; www.brooklynX.org. Information on culture, shopping, history, local parks and events.
● Queens Council on the Arts, 79-01 Park Lane South, Woodhaven, NY 11421, tel: 718-291-ARTS (2787).
● Staten Island Tourism Council, 1 Edgewater Plaza, Staten Island, NY 10305, tel: 718-442 4356; 1-800 573 7469. Useful facts on cultural events and places of interest. It also maintains an information kiosk in the Ferry Terminal at Battery Park in Manhattan.

Useful Websites

In addition to the websites in the A–Z part of this book and the borough sites listed under "Useful Addresses, " the following websites also provide information:
● www.newyork.citysearch.com for events, restaurants and shopping.
● www.newyork.today.com for social news, offered by *The New York Times*.
● www.queens.nyc.ny.us for information on cultural attractions in Queens.
● www.ny.com for a broad range of information from car rentals, shopping and sports to news and weather updates.

Activities for Children

Most sightseeing activities that adults might take part in are likely to appeal to children, especially the Circle Line boat trip around Manhattan, Macy's Thanksgiving Day parade, the July 4th fireworks display over the East River, and visits to the Statue of Liberty and the Empire State Building. Some supposedly adult activities, such as visiting the Fulton Fish Market at six o'clock in the morning, might even appeal more to children than to their parents. Central Park has an entire children's area, including a

children's zoo, an antique carousel and a marionette theater. Saturday morning story-telling takes place in summertime by the statue of Hans Christian Andersen near the Conservatory Water (East 74th Street), which is also a very good spot to go model boat racing.

There's a wonderful children's zoo in Brooklyn's Prospect Park; hundreds of exotic fish for kids to wonder at in the New York Aquarium, West Eighth Street and Surf Avenue, Coney Island; while the Bronx Zoo is worth an entire day's adventure. At the American Museum of Natural History, Central Park West and 79th Street, the dinosaur collection is always popular. Not far away, the Children's Museum of Manhattan at 212 West 83rd Street encourages hands-on participation – though the noise level might encourage ear-plugs.

The Oldest Children's Museum

There's a similar hands-on museum at Snug Harbor in Staten Island, while the Brooklyn Children's Museum at 145 Brooklyn Avenue is the country's oldest. You may also want to consider the New York City Fire Museum, 278 Spring Street, while

Above: Barbie for President

strolling through SoHo; the dazzling Liberty Science Center (just across the Hudson River, in New Jersey), or the South Street Seaport's Children's Center.

There are playgrounds throughout the city, including Central Park; Washington Square Park; at West 74th Street and Riverside Drive; at Second Avenue and 93rd Street; and in Queens, where the New York Hall of Science in Flushing Meadows-Corona Park not only has the largest outdoor science playground in the US but also features more than 100 indoor "experiments" for children to work on.

Facilities for the Disabled

Disabled travelers can obtain information about rights, facilities, special access and hotels that cater to people with disabilities by writing to the Mayor's Office for People with Disabilities, 52 Chambers St, Room 206, New York, NY 10007, tel: 788 2830.

Above: city kids in the park

Gay New York

Gays are welcome pretty much everywhere in New York, but special stomping grounds include the West Village around Christopher Street, and some of the bars and cafes in Chelsea. Special events include the Gay and Lesbian Pride Day Parade on Fifth Avenue (June), when the Empire State Building turns sympathetic colors, and the outrageous Halloween Parade in Greenwich Village (Oct).

The Gay and Lesbian Switchboard, tel: 989 0999, exists specifically to provide information to men and women about all aspects of gay life in New York including recommendations of bars, restaurants, accommodations, legal counseling, etc. The Lesbian and Gay Community Services Center, 208 West 13th Street, tel: 620 7310, is another helpful organization. Bookshops such as A Different Light, 151 West 19th Street and the Oscar Wilde Memorial Bookshop at 15 Christopher Street stock various useful publications.

Shopping

Shopping is a major pastime in New York, and the choice is vast. For culture buffs, art is always a good bet; apart from the major auctioneers, Sotheby's and Christies – where record prices are set for world-famous works – there are hundreds of art galleries in which to browse (if not to buy).

These are found all over town, but it's most fun to stroll

Above: steppin' out **Right:** *innovative marketing*

through SoHo on a Saturday to see, not only what's on sale, but also all the shows in the lofts and galleries.

Antiques can be found in Greenwich Village along Bleecker Street and on side streets off University Place; along upper Madison Avenue, on 60th Street near Third Avenue; and on Lafayette Street below Houston Street, as well as at a few indoor "malls" around the city, including the Manhattan Art & Antiques Center, 1050 Second Avenue; Metropolitan Art & Antiques Pavilion, 110 West 19th Street; and the Chelsea Antiques Building, 110 West 25th Street.

Famous Department Stores

The city's department stores offer something for everyone. The most famous are Bloomingdale's (1000 Third Avenue at 59th Street) and Macy's (151 West 34th Street), which sell everything from housewares to furniture and clothing. Lord & Taylor (424 Fifth Avenue at 39th Street) and Saks Fifth Avenue (611 Fifth Avenue) concentrate on clothes, with Saks offering the most upscale fashions. SoHo and the Upper East Side are where the

highest proportion of classy clothing boutiques can be found, with Madison Avenue thick with expensive possibilities.

There's another stretch of elegance along Fifth Avenue from Rockefeller Center to the Plaza Hotel, with Takashimaya (693 Fifth Avenue), Henri Bendel (712 Fifth Avenue), Prada (724 Fifth Avenue) and Bergdorf Goodman (754 Fifth Avenue) briefly interrupted by a burst of mass merchandising at 57th Street.

Electronic and photographic suppliers can be found almost everywhere, including Times Square and on Lexington Avenue near Grand Central. A few outlets can be less than scrupulous, however, and have been known to prey on tourists, so it's best to do some comparison shopping before actually buying. A better bet might be in the downtown City Hall district or on Fifth Avenue between 37th and 40th streets.

Street markets include the weekend Chelsea Antiques Market (Sixth Avenue, 25th–27th streets) and the Sunday Flea Market at Columbus Avenue and 77th Street on the Upper West Side.

Above: *the city that shops till it drops*

And now for the big picture...

The text you have been reading is extracted from *Insight Guide: New York City*, one of 200 titles in the award-winning Insight Guides series. Its 300 pages are packed with expert essays covering New York's history and culture, detailed itineraries for the entire city, a comprehensive listings section, a full set of clear, cross-referenced maps, and hundreds of great photographs. It's an inspiring background read, an invaluable on-the-spot companion, and a superb souvenir of a visit. Available from all good bookshops.

Also from Insight Guides...

Insight Guides is the award-winning classic series that provides the complete picture of a destination, with expert and informative text and the world's best photography. Each book has everything you need, being an ideal travel planner, a reliable on-the-spot guide, and a superb souvenir of a trip. Nearly 200 titles.

Insight Maps are designed to complement the guidebooks. They provide full, clear mapping of major destinations, list top sights, and their laminated finish makes them durable and easy to fold. More than 100 titles.

Insight Compact Guides are handy reference books, modestly priced but comprehensive. Text, pictures and maps are all cross-referenced, making them ideal books for on-the-spot use. 120 titles.

Insight Pocket Guides pioneered the concept of the authors as "local hosts" who provide personal recommendations, just as they would give honest advice to a friend. Pull-out map included. 120 titles.

INSIGHT GUIDES

The world's largest collection of visual travel guides